# MORNINGS with JENKINS

### THE TALE OF A SUCCESSFUL LEADER

JEAN YARGER

Mornings with Jenkins

*The Tale of a Successful Leader*
*By Jean Yarger*

Copyright © 2012 by Jean Yarger. All rights reserved. No part of this book may be reproduced in any form or by any electronic or mechanical means including information storage and retrieval system without permission in writing from the author, except by a reviewer who may quote brief passages in a review.

Printed in the United States

**Fine Pointe Publishing**

W71N391 Cedar Pointe Ave
Cedarburg, WI 53012 U.S.A.

ISBN: 1468199811
ISBN-13: 9781468199819

Yarger, Jean;
Mornings with Jenkins:
The Tale of a Successful Leader

To my sons – thank you for the encouragement

To Jim – Thank you for the opportunity.

# Contents

**Preface – What's the Question?** . . . . . . . . . . . . . . . . . . ix

**Morning One, Vision** . . . . . . . . . . . . . . . . . . . . . . . . 1
    1. Weeds and Pests
    2. What To Communicate

**Morning Two, Values** . . . . . . . . . . . . . . . . . . . . . . . 15
    1. Birds of a Feather
    2. Observe Behavior

**Morning Three, Trust** . . . . . . . . . . . . . . . . . . . . . . . 29
    1. Too Far From the Woodpile
    2. Limit the Issues

**Morning Four, Priorities** . . . . . . . . . . . . . . . . . . . . . 41
    1. Acorn Lesson
    2. Measure Commitment

**Morning Five, Assumptions** . . . . . . . . . . . . . . . . . . . 55
    1. Most Wonderful Day
    2. How to Communicate

**Morning Six, Leadership** . . . . . . . . . . . . . . . . . . . . . 71

**Quick Tips in a Nutshell** . . . . . . . . . . . . . . . . . . . . . 75

*Leadership –*

*helping people find new depths of ability through your vision.*

# Preface
# What's the Question?

This book was written for anyone who lives or works with another human being and wants to replace confused, fearful, ambiguous talking with rational, defensible, meaningful communication.

I was involved in the start-up of a small pharmaceutical manufacturing company. The management team was comprised of highly trained, intelligent people who could assess scientific data and solve the most complicated chemical equation. But when it came to people problems, most of our managers were totally lost.

The consensus among the management team was do good science and the people problems will take care of themselves. But our company was growing and with each new hire came more people issues. Managers were complaining about poor performance, no sense of urgency and a lack of responsibility. We discussed ways to approach issues, revised our performance management system and implemented a pay for performance policy. We brought in numerous consultants to help us manage the growth. One particular consultant was brought in to help develop leadership. He was very engaging, relating interesting stories and examples of good leadership. The message was that good leaders communicate by giving clear directives, requiring accountability and never rationalizing poor performance. The management team enjoyed the presentation and all commented that they found his delivery to be entertaining - but none of them grasped the idea that leadership requires focused and consistent communication.

# MORNINGS WITH JENKINS

The morning after the leadership training I took a cup of coffee and a copy of the presentation out to the patio. Usually it is just me and the birds at this early hour. But this particular morning there was a rabbit under the birdfeeder eating weeds sprouting from discarded birdseed. I was enjoying the quiet and contemplating how difficult communication is when I noticed two chipmunks running across the patio. When the chipmunks noticed me they stopped for a moment as if to say, "Ssssh", then quietly snuck up on the rabbit. The rabbit was so startled he jumped a foot straight up off the ground. This little encounter made me smile and I thought, "I've worked with people like you."

Can leaders require accountability? People create so many problems and issues. People make assumptions about what they see and hear. They make excuses and blame others for their mistakes. And then they share their assumptions and interpretations. When communication is driven by assumptions and interpretation, it is difficult to identify the real issue and hold people accountable.

I was absentmindedly watching the rabbit eating sprouts under the bird feeder. This rabbit never ate the flowers I had carefully planted around the patio, which got me to wondering. Why would anyone choose to sacrifice personal wants for the well being of the organization?

Our management team could not agree on a single message, therefore people were interpreting directives based on their personal needs and what had been allowed in the past. In fact, we had department managers who felt that their departmental function was more important than other departments. The company was being lead in multiple directions.

Suddenly those two chipmunks were sitting right under my chair. Quickly I pulled my feet up onto the chair and watched as those little rodents defiantly marched over to the bird feeder and began eating sprouts. This time the rabbit jumped on them and chased them away. The message was very clear, even to a human like me. Sprouts are for rabbits. That rabbit assessed performance held the chipmunks accountable and gave clear directives all within a few seconds.

How was it that a rabbit could communicate so confidently and effectively? As far as I was concerned, eating sprouts is not more important than eating seeds. Both activities keep weeds from growing under the birdfeeder. Evidently, these responsibilities had been defined by the critters in the Garden. Rabbits are responsible

## WHAT'S THE QUESTION?

for the sprouts. Chipmunks are responsible for the seeds. Maybe the chipmunks were just playing another joke on the rabbit. Maybe there were fewer seeds and more sprouts that day. But this rabbit did not let excuses keep him from addressing their behavior. He knew it was his responsibility to correct the behavior, and in doing so, the chipmunks' responsibilities were defined.

A rabbit communicated simply, confidently, effectively and, I might add, efficiently. The chipmunks went right back to eating seeds. So why is it so hard for humans? Our managers made excuses for people. They found it hard to separate the person from the behavior. Management allowed the blame game to cloud the real issues and rationalized unacceptable behavior in some individuals. In doing so, they lost focus.

Whether you are a CEO, department manager, committee chair or Cub Scout leader, the success of your organization is dependent on your ability to communicate quickly, confidently and effectively. But to be a confident, effective leader you need to know what and how to communicate. To respond quickly, you must recognize when you are communicating. To become a good leader, the question is what, how and when to communicate. It does not have to take a lot of time. It is not some special leadership gene that only a few are born with. In fact, it's so simple a rabbit showed me how.

# Morning One Vision

I had been awake most of the night, worrying. Afraid that my tossing and turning would wake my wife, I slipped out of bed and down the stairs. Five a.m. How much longer could I hang on? If I could not turn things around, I was going to lose the company I started. I made a cup of coffee and stepped outside to our patio. The sun was just rising. There was a chill in the air. The patio was still and calm, but I felt nothing but panic. Was it worth it? When did I lose control? How do I fix this – do I want to?

I found myself staring at my neighbor's garden. We had a yard. The neighbor had a Garden. It was so well planned and cared for. Her Garden was a picture of beauty and peace. Everything was healthy and blooming. I walked to the edge of my yard to get a better look. Sitting in the sun on the warm stone patio was a chubby, fluffy rabbit. Sure, I thought, you eat my flowers and then take a nap in the neighbor's Garden. Then I noticed the neighbor sitting at her patio table, writing. Not wanting to disturb her I turned to go back to my patio when the neighbor called.

"Good Morning, John! You're up early."

"So are you," I called.

"Jenkins and I love this time of day. It is so peaceful. It is a great time to reflect and organize our thoughts," she said.

# MORNINGS WITH JENKINS

Because I spent most of my time working, I was not very familiar with my neighbors. I knew Jean was the owner of this beautiful Garden. Until now our conversations consisted of hellos and comments on the weather. I was not sure who Jenkins was — husband, maybe?

"You look as though you could use another cup of coffee." She waved at the pot sitting on the table. "I have plenty."

"Is it that obvious?" I asked.

"Well, usually you have left for work by now," smiled Jean.

I was still in my pajamas and should have been getting to work but instead I walked over to Jean's Garden. I have no idea why, but I found myself sitting on Jean's patio, drinking her coffee and sharing my problems. "I just don't get it," I said. "Why don't my employees take responsibility? They're all so busy blaming each other, me or the customer, that nothing gets done. They say one thing and do another. They're all so worried about themselves. There is no commitment to the organization."

Jean poured more coffee into my cup. "I'm sorry. I didn't mean to dump all this on you," I said.

"This is exactly why I created the Garden," said Jean. "Please stay, John. It is the most important thing you could be doing right now. I have been where you are. If you are going to rescue your organization, you need to get in touch with why you started it in the first place."

I sank back into the chair on Jean's patio. Why did I start this company? It sure doesn't look anything like the company I had envisioned. How did I get so far off track? I leaned back and closed my eyes.

"Leading a company and managing an organization is difficult. There is much to do and many details. It is easy to get off track. As the organization grows, or as the economy fluctuates, opportunities and problems present themselves. What provides stability and direction in your company?" asked Jean.

"Well, we have a strategic plan." I was wondering where this was going.

"How do you know if the strategic plan has succeeded?" She asked.

This was getting a little frustrating. "We look at the bottom line."

"The financial statements," Jean asked, and then went on without waiting for an answer. "It is easy to manage the functions of the business. Functions create definable data that result in financial statements. The financial statements are a definitive picture of the financial health of the organization. But, the financial statements are the result of how people performed in those business functions. If you are managing business functions and waiting for the financial statements to be published before making strategic decisions, you're managing history. You will never recognize what people are doing right now that affect, negatively or positively, next year's financial statements."

I must have looked puzzled because Jean went on.

"We communicate all day long whether we know it or not. We communicate equally by what we say – and what we don't say. What we do and what we don't do. The only way to control what is communicated is to define and focus on the message." Then Jean asked me, "How can you give clear directives if you do not know what your goals and priorities are, John?"

Jean did not wait for an answer. "How can you hold people accountable if you do not know what your expectations are?"

I opened my eyes to discover the rabbit had moved and was sitting under Jean's chair and looking directly at me. "I'm sorry, what were you saying?"

"What is your Vision for the company? What are your goals, priorities and expectations, John?"

"Oh, we have been down that road," I answered. "We hired an advisor to come in. We had all the V.P.s and managers work on developing a Vision. I am not sure where we put that."

Jean poured herself another cup of coffee. "The Vision is at the core of an organization's existence. The Vision begins the strategic planning process. Without it there is no direction. Trying to run a company without a Vision is like trying to navigate without a compass. Without direction, the best the organization can do is run aimlessly. The worst the company can do is sink and go out of business."

I had never thought about Vision in this way. Jean went on, "the Vision tells your employees, customers and the community who your company is, what it does and why it does it. The Vision is what you should be talking about. When the Vision is the compass for developing strategy and the standard for judging individual and organizational performance, expectations are more easily defined. The Vision becomes the ruler against which performance is measured."

The rabbit was looking at me with such interest it was making me uncomfortable. "Your Garden is truly beautiful. When we do dishes, we look out at your Garden from our kitchen window," I said as I got up to leave. "I have one question. Why don't the rabbits eat your flowers? They've eaten just about everything in our yard."

"Well, that is an interesting story," chuckled Jean. "I think I'll let Jenkins tell it."

Thinking I was going to meet her husband I asked, "Your husband?"

Jean pointed to the Rabbit under her chair.

# *Weeds and Pests*

Hello, are you enjoying the Garden? I hope I am not disturbing you. It truly is a peaceful and restful place. But that is no accident! It takes hard work and dedication to maintain a beautiful Garden. A lot of damage can be done in short order if you are not constantly on the watch.

Take, for example, this Garden. This was not always beautiful Garden. It used to be an empty field, just wide open space. Creatures passed through, but no one made their home here. There were no trees or bushes to hide in and make a home. There were, however, a lot of rocks and boulders. Food was not plentiful. I use to hop through this field upon occasion, trying to find something to eat.

Oh, I am sorry. Please forgive me. I have not introduced myself. My name is Jenkins. Yes, your eyes do not deceive you. I am a rabbit. You see, Jean gave me my name and this Garden was Jean's Vision. She once told me that she created the Garden to provide a beautiful, safe and peaceful home for all creatures that are willing to share and maintain the Garden. It was her hard work and persistence that created this Garden and I am proud to call it home.

Do you have a moment? This is an unusual story. One day, as I was hopping through the field, I noticed a human moving rocks and pulling up the few good plants that grew here. Well, of course I thought, "There goes the neighborhood. There will be nothing left for me to eat."

I continued to hop by from time to time and noticed a human planting some delectable looking plants that were unfamiliar to me. There were so many different colors and shapes. And the smell! It was a rabbit smorgasbord. I could not resist. I just had to taste these wonderful plants. I ventured closer. The human looked at me and smiled, "Hello, welcome to my Garden. My name is Jean. Are you friend or pest?"

Not having much experience with human creatures, I cautiously ventured toward a delectable looking blue flower. "Oh, I see. You're a pest. You're not welcome if you're going to eat my flowers", Jean said.

Pest? I had no idea what that meant but I did not think I wanted to be a pest. Jean continued. "I do not mind if you eat the weeds but please leave the flowers alone."

Weeds? Flowers? I saw food. I slowly hopped away. But I could not stay away. I just had to get a taste of one of those blue flowers. I returned in the early morning. I tried again in the late afternoon. It did not seem to matter when I hopped by, Jean was always very busy tending her Garden. I tried hopping very slowly. I tried being very quiet. I tried being very still, that usually works with dogs. But Jean always saw me and would chase me out of her Garden. She assumed, correctly I might add, that I was after her blue flowers.

I noticed that birds and bees were allowed to eat her flowers. In fact there were all kinds of birds and insects in her Garden. Even a couple of chipmunks and a mouse played near the wood pile. They were never chased away.

One morning I happened to get into the Garden before Jean. This was my chance! I finished one especially delectable blue flower and was enjoying a second, when all of a sudden Jean was right beside me with a broom. "Get out of my Garden! You are destroying my hard work! Get out and do not ever come back!"

I scurried just beyond the Garden and turned to see if Jean was chasing me. She was bending down to look at the plant I had eaten. She looked up at me. "If I allow you to eat the flowers what will the hummingbirds and bees eat?"

Yeah, but what about me, I thought, what will I eat? Still I had never seen Jean so angry. Obviously the Garden meant more to her than I did.

For several days I hopped past Jean's Garden but did not stop. I saw Jean working and Jean saw me. She would stand up and look at me as if she did not trust me. I did not like that feeling.

# WEEDS AND PESTS

One morning, I found myself sitting at the edge of Jean's Garden. I could not help myself. It was so beautiful and peaceful. All the creatures seemed so happy and safe. I had not noticed Jean sitting on the patio watching me. When I finally saw Jean she smiled. "All creatures are welcome as long as they value the Garden."

Jean stood up and walked over to the bird feeder. She kneeled down and began pulling plants up from the ground. This was something new. Usually she was putting plants into the ground. I slowly hopped toward the feeder. The plants had sprouted from bird seed that had fallen from the bird feeder.

Jean smiled at me. "These plants volunteer to grow here. They are weeds and they detract from the Garden."

To me they looked like tasty young sprouts. I took a nibble and Jean smiled. "You need a name. Do you like Jenkins? I am going to call you Jenkins."

From that day on, Jean and I spent quiet, early mornings together on the patio - Jean with a cup of coffee and me with the tasty sprouts under the bird feeder. We discussed which flowers should be planted and the many creatures that were choosing to make the Garden their home. I was beginning to understand the difference between weeds and flowers. I felt safe and pleased that Jean trusted me.

One day, I woke from my midday nap in the buttercups, to find a rabbit acquaintance eating the blue flowers. Jean was nowhere in sight. I did not want her seeing some of the blue flowers missing and thinking I had eaten them. I began yelling to the rabbit, "Stop that! Do not eat the blue flowers! Jean will be very angry!"

The rabbit look up at me. "What's your problem? Want these yummy plants all to yourself?"

"No, no, that's not it. The blue flowers are for the hummingbirds and bees. Jean will be very angry and not let me live here anymore if she thinks I ate them." I was very upset with this rabbit. He was not paying any attention to me. He just went right on, eating the blue flowers.

"Stop! Stop right now!" I yelled. I could not believe my own ears. Here I was yelling at a fellow rabbit. He was just hungry. But I was committed to Jean's Garden. I just could not let him eat the flowers. I tried to distract him. "Look, over by the bird feeder there are some delightful young sprouts. That is what I eat. Please join me for a bite."

"There is not enough for two rabbits over there. These blue flowers are the best-tasting thing I have ever had." This rabbit was very stubborn. "Besides, why do you care what the hummingbirds and bees eat?" He asked.

Why, indeed. I suddenly realized it was not just because I didn't want to be blamed for eating the blue flowers. The Garden had become more important to me than what I ate. Every creature that lives here contributes to the Garden. I had come to respect how the hummingbirds and bees help the flowers and plants grow. I was not going to let this rabbit eat their food.

I chased that rabbit out of the Garden and told him to never return. I guess that must have been quite the sight, because when I turned around, Jean was standing on the patio with her broom - laughing.

# What to Communicate

The business plan describes the opportunity. It presents facts that support the need for what the organization will provide and projects financial returns. It is a document designed to remove emotion and present facts to investors and leaders to facilitate an informed financial decision.

The Vision statement is a description of what the organization will look like when it succeeds. It is influenced by experience, beliefs and interpretations. It does not dictate every decision or demand a particular action. The Vision is not a "how to" or "paint by number". It is a vivid impression, painted with broad strokes and leaves little doubt as to what success looks like. The Vision must be so clear that priorities are never in question, so simple that responsibilities are never in doubt, and so well defined that threats to the organization are quickly identified. At the same time it must not be so restrictive that people cannot respond to change and grow with opportunity. The Vision is the stabilizer when economic events create instability. It is the compass when the customer's needs change or technology creates new opportunities. It sets parameters for what is acceptable and what is not acceptable. The key to creating and sharing a Vision lies in how the Vision is developed and used.

## DEVELOPING A VISION STATEMENT

The process for developing a Vision statement forces leadership to define the assumptions on which the Vision is based, and strategies for how the Vision will be achieved. A Vision development chart is a very useful tool for defining and prioritizing assumptions

## Step One: Define Assumptions

People want to believe and feel pride in what they are doing. The assumptions individuals make as to why they do their job, what their job is and who they do their job for, will determine their performance. Every Vision is built on the assumptions of the person or people who develop the Vision. Clarity can occur only when assumptions are limited and defined. There are only three assumptions that must be defined when developing a Vision statement; who the organization is, what the organization does, why the organization does it. To define these assumptions, there are three questions that must be answered.

1. ***What is the organization's goal?***

    Asking what the goal is defines who the organization is. It defines the singular goal for all employees. There are no other goals. Each department and individual contributes to this singular goal.

2. ***What does the organization contribute?***

    The contributions that the organization makes differentiate and define what the organization does. It describes what it offers and what it does that makes it unique. Defining the contribution that the organization makes creates focus and purpose.

3. ***What does the organization help others do?***

    What the organization helps others do, defines why the organization does it and who they do it for. This creates pride in the organization and establishes priorities.

To develop a vision, begin with a Vision Development Chart. The chart should have three columns, one column for each of the three questions listed above. In the column below each question, write every answer you can think of for each of the questions.

## VISION DEVELOPMENT CHART

| What is the organization's goal? (Who are we?) | What contributions does the organization make? (What do we do?) | What does the organization help others achieve? (Why do we do it?) |
|---|---|---|
|  |  |  |

## *Step Two: Prioritize*

There will be multiple answers for each of the questions, some more important than others. Which statement in each column is the most important? Prioritizing the answers from most important to least is a critical step. Defining what is most important now will allow you to recognize when people have lost focus or are working on the wrong thing later.

## *Step Three: Compose*

Using the most important answers to each question, write your Vision statement answering who you are, what you do, why you do it.

## USING THE VISION

Personal visions must align with the organization's vision for the organization to succeed. Take for example the pharmaceutical manufacturer with the following vision:

> *Our company is a contract manufacturer of active pharmaceutical ingredients (API), developing, improving and manufacturing quality products for the pharmaceutical industry.*

The manager of the Research and Development Department was asked to write a vision statement for his department. It read:

> *The Research and Development Department provides research and development expertise that improves manufacturing processes for API.*

Place the two Visions side by side, and obvious discrepancies are observed.

|  | **Organization** | **Research and Development Department** |
|---|---|---|
| **Who we are** | Contract manufacturer of active pharmaceutical ingredients | Research and Development Department |
| **What we do** | Research, develop and improve processes, and manufacture quality products | Provides research and development expertise |
| **Why we do it** | For the pharmaceutical industry. | Improves manufacturing processes of active pharmaceutical ingredients |

The company's goal is to make money by contracting with pharmaceutical companies to manufacture quality API. The R&D Department goal is to provide research and development expertise that will result in improved processes.

The company is assuming that an improved process will result in reduced costs and higher quality product that they can sell at a competitive price. While the R&D department is assuming that an optimized processes is what the company is selling. It may seem very subtle, but the results of not clarifying this assumption will be devastating.

Research and Development is not the company. They are the research and development part of the company. The research and development department provides research and development services so the company can make money. Everyone should be working toward the organization's goal. There are no other goals. When a department's goals become more important than the organization's goals, it builds a silo around itself. The result will be over budget and late delivery of projects and plenty of excuses and blame.

# Morning Two Values

Saturday morning! I had been waiting for this day all week. Things had calmed down a little at work so I decided to take a Saturday off and help my wife with the yard. I gathered all the tools and marched to the back yard. Jenkins was sunning himself on Jean's patio. "Good morning Jenkins! Where is Jean? Don't tell me she hasn't come out yet!" I was priding myself on being the first one up.

Just then Jean came around the corner of her house. "Good morning, John. Big plans today?" She nodded to the tools I was holding.

"Yes," I replied. "Do you suppose I could impose on Jenkins to get the rabbits to stop eating my flowers?"

Jenkins lifted his head and looked at me as if to say "Thank you, no, I have enough to do in this Garden," Jean laughed. "How is work going?"

"Interesting you should ask," I replied. "I did not go into work the morning I had coffee with you. I spent the rest of the day defining my Vision. The next day, I went into work and removed the framed Vision statement from the conference room wall. That Vision statement had always bothered me. It just did not capture my original Vision. But we had grown rather quickly and needed to rally the troops, so we hired a consultant and spent a lot of money developing a Vision statement and hung it on the wall."

Jean looked surprised. "What happened after you took it down?"

MORNINGS WITH JENKINS

"I called my direct reports together. I told them the story of why I started my company and described what success looked like to me. I explained who we are, what we do and who we do it for. Then I hung my new Vision statement on the wall. You know, I don't think anyone had noticed that the old Vision statement was missing until then."

"How did that go over?" Jean sat down and motion for me to join her.

I wandered over to Jean's patio and said. "I went on to explain that from now on there was only one parameter for judging performance – commitment to that Vision."

Jean chuckled. "How many people quit?"

"Well, I have to admit it was met with mixed reviews. Some felt they should have had some input. Others did not agree with it at all. Never the less, I kept to my plan. In every meeting I've been thanking people for specific actions or events that have shown commitment to the organization. When someone says they don't think something is possible, I remind them that what we do is important and our customers depend on us. And when I see people working on the wrong thing I ask, 'Is that the most important thing to be doing right now?'

Taking a sip of coffee Jean asked, "Is everyone on board?"

"Oh - people are slowly getting on board. More importantly, I feel rested enough to tackle our yard. My wife is thrilled!"

I was getting up to go back to my work when Jean asked, "Have you thought about what you value?"

"What do you mean," I asked?

"You know, what is really important to the organization? For example, in the Garden we value peace and safety."

I scratched my head. "O.K. So…"

"It's just that now you have defined your Vision, how are you going to measure commitment to it?"

Measure commitment? Maybe I needed more coffee. I could not for the life of me figure out where this was going.

"People, who do not value what you value, are not committed to the organization. You'll never recognize potentially damaging behaviors, or take effective corrective action, if you have not defined your values ."

This woman could be exasperating. The look on my face did not deter her from asking, "Do you have a few more minutes? Jenkins had a very interesting experience this week."

# Birds of a Feather

We had a very sad experience in the Garden. In fact, I learned a very difficult lesson. It all began with Raven. Raven is one of the largest birds to ever visit the Garden. His is a commanding presence, all dressed in sleek, shiny black feathers. When he comes to the Garden, most of the birds and smaller animals return to their homes and watch with respect. I often thought he seemed to be a lonely bird.

Sammy Sparrow and his friends are the only birds I had ever seen play with Raven. They seemed to play a game of tag high in the sky, which Raven always won.

One day I asked Sammy Sparrow what kind of game he played with Raven. "Game! Jenkins, that is no game!" Sammy replied. "We must keep Raven out of Jean's Garden!"

This response surprised me. "But everyone is welcome in Jean's Garden," I reminded Sammy.

"Raven will disturb the peace," said Sammy. "We cannot allow Raven into our garden!"

I thought hard, but I could not recall a time when Raven had ever disturbed the peace. So I asked Sammy why he thought these things about Raven.

"Well," Sammy replied. "My Mother has always told me that Raven is very dangerous. She taught me to chase and pester Raven and never allow him to land in our Garden."

"Yes, but have you ever actually witnessed Raven disturbing the peace?" I asked.

# MORNINGS WITH JENKINS

"Well, no, I have not seen it with my own eyes," Sammy considered thoughtfully. "But, that is because we sparrows patrol the Garden and do not allow him to land."

This just did not make sense to me, so I asked Sammy how one bird could dislike another bird.

"There are differences in birds, you see. We do not all look the same or eat the same things. Some of us cannot even fly," Sammy explained. "All sparrows are birds but not all birds are sparrows." Then, Sammy flew away.

At the time, I thought that was a strange statement, but I forgot all about that conversation - until just the other day.

Mr. and Mrs. Robin had been very busy building their nest since returning early this spring. We had not spoken since last summer. That is not unusual. Mr. and Mrs. Robin are always very busy. From the time they arrive until their chicks leave the nest, they flutter and fly about, first building their nest, next taking care of their eggs, and then feeding their chicks. Between the time their eggs arrive and the chicks hatch, they have a little more time to chat.

It was on such a day that I saw Mrs. Robin sitting on a branch of the evergreen tree near her nest.

"Good morning, Mrs. Robin. How are you this fine morning?" I asked.

"It is a fine morning!" she chirped. "We are all well, thank you."

"We?" I asked. "How many eggs this year?"

"We have four," she stated proudly.

Robin eggs are the most delicate blue eggs you will ever see. They are small and totally dependent on Mr. and Mrs. Robin. For several weeks, Mr. and Mrs. Robin take turns sitting on the nest to keep the eggs warm until they hatch.

"Four eggs – you must be so proud. Congratulations!" I exclaimed.

Just then Raven appeared. He flew into the evergreen tree, knocking Mrs. Robin off her perch. The Robin nest teetered, then crashed to the ground.

"Hey!" I demanded. "Hey, Raven! Stop that! What are you doing?"

"I am getting my lunch," Raven responded matter-of-factly.

Just then the sparrows flew in and chased Raven away. Mrs. Robin lay on the ground, with an injured wing. Her nest was in tatters around her, and the eggs were gone! Mr. Robin landed quickly beside her and tried his best to console her.

"I am so sorry," I said. "I had no idea one bird could do that to another bird."

"I have heard of such things," sobbed Mrs. Robin, "but I never thought it could happen in Jean's Garden."

"We will leave Jean's Garden at once!" declared Mr. Robin.

"Oh, please don't leave," I begged. "You have been such good neighbors. Please don't leave."

"We are afraid. How can we possibly stay? What if Raven returns?" the Robins exclaimed.

"What if I can assure you that this will never happen again?" I asked. "Will you stay, then?"

"But how can you promise that?" squeaked Sammy as he returned from chasing Raven away. "Didn't you see what just happened?" Sammy was tapping his foot on the ground. I had never seen him so angry.

"See? Yes! Just terrible, terrible! How can you promise we are going to be safe? Yes, safe! The peace has been broken. We are scared!" All the animals were chattering at once.

This single event had changed Jean's Garden in an instant. I looked around to see that all of the creatures who had been living peacefully in the Garden were either hiding or fleeing, afraid that it would happen again.

"Please, please, let me try to talk to Raven," I begged.

"Talk to Raven? I doubt that will do any good." Sammy's mother had just landed on a branch of the evergreen tree.

"Why not?" I asked.

Mr. and Mrs. Robin squealed nervously. "Well, just look at him. He is so big. And you can't see his eyes. They are the same color as his feathers. You can't trust someone whose eyes are the same color as his feathers. Yes, that's right. You just can't trust him."

Mr. and Mrs. Robin had returned to their tree and were assessing the damage. "Besides," they added, "look what he did!"

I could not argue with that. "Why do you think he did it?" I asked them.

"BECAUSE RAVEN IS MEAN!" they yelled in unison.

"That's it? He was born mean?" I challenged their logic. "He just likes hurting other birds because his eyes are the same color as his feathers? Or because he is big?" I was angry. "Is that what you honestly think?"

"Well, what do you propose we do?" demanded Sammy.

I thought for a moment. "I am going to invite him to tea." And that is just what I did.

The day Raven joined me for tea all the other creatures were hiding. Everyone refused to join us. I welcomed Raven. "Raven, I am so glad you accepted my invitation."

"I must admit that I was intrigued by your invitation," replied Raven. "I do not receive many invitations to tea, and I wanted to see what you would serve."

"Were you expecting robin eggs?" I asked.

"I was hoping. They are a delicacy," said Raven, "and my favorite food."

"Is that why you destroyed Mr. and Mrs. Robin's nest?"

"I never really thought about it," Raven responded. "I just love eggs."

"Raven," I started carefully, "as long as you eat robin eggs, I do not think that you will be invited to many tea parties."

"What do you mean, Jenkins?" Raven asked sincerely.

I explained that in Jean's Garden, creatures do not eat each other's eggs and that if he did not respect the eggs, he simply was not welcome in Jean's Garden.

"This is a fine how-do-you-do," Raven protested. "I thought all creatures were welcome in Jean's Garden."

I thought so too until that moment. It made me a little sad. All Sparrows are birds, but not all birds are Sparrows.

# Observe Behavior

It is not enough to produce elegant Vision statements. The Vision must be put into action. How the Vision is implemented dictates how the organization will be remembered. Values define how the organization expects people to behave.

People are communicating all the time, even when they do not think they are communicating. The most meaningful communication is not in what is said but what is done. How people behave is evidence of their understanding and level of commitment to the Vision. Behavior is the strongest and most effective form of communication. What people say and what they do are often two different things. People who say they agree or understand and then proceed to do the opposite are committed to their personal interests. People who are willing to put the organization's needs before their personal interests are committed to the organization. The proof is in what they do. You do not know what the other person is really thinking until you see them in action.

Some difficult questions arise when defining Values. For example, which is more important to you?

- Honesty or trying to be the best?

- People enjoying their job or people getting the job done no matter what it takes?

- The deadline or the quality of the work?

Most people will answer it depends on the situation. But does it really?

## HOW DO YOU BEHAVE?

- Do you blame the customer's indecisions for the tight timeframe or are you honest with employees about why you decided to take on this project?

- Do you meet deadlines and worry about quality later or do you stop the process and correct quality issues and try to find ways to make up the time?

- Are you consistent or do you consider some people too important and allow them to live outside the organization's Values?

A leader's strongest communication tool is their personal behavior. When they take action and what causes them to take action tells everyone in the organization what is important, what is allowed and what is not. *Remember, leadership's behavior identifies what is important. What you do says a lot more about what you value than what you say.*

The process of defining Values requires that choices be made and creates consistency. For example in the Garden is it more important:

> For the Garden to be safe or beautiful?

> All creatures are allowed in - or that the creatures who live there contribute to the Garden?

The Garden's Vision states:

*"The Garden is a safe home for all creatures willing to contribute to the beauty and peace of the Garden."*

There is plenty of room for interpretation. What is beauty? What is a contribution? Defining how the organization will be remembered places the focus on behaviors, and what commitment looks like.

## THE GARDEN'S VISION DEVELOPMENT CHART

| What is the organization's goal? | What does the organization contribute? | What does the organization help others achieve? | How will the organization be remembered? |
|---|---|---|---|
| To be a Garden | A home | Helps others live safely | A safe home |
| To be a beautiful place | The beauty of the neighborhood | Helps others rest | For beauty and peace |
| To be a restful place | A place for reflection | Help others learn to reflect and succeed. | For helping others succeed |

The goal of the Garden is to be a Garden. It is not a park or a meadow. It is in the business of being a Garden. The Garden's contribution is homes for creatures. If this were a business, it would make money by selling homes. What it helps others achieve is safety, beauty and peace. This Garden will be remembered for being a safe, beautiful and restful place. The members of the Garden must behave in ways that contribute to the safety, beauty and peace of the Garden.

When Values have been clearly and consistently communicated, people know what their response will be and confidently take action, even in the most difficult situations. When Values are inconsistently communicated there will be conflict. People cannot stay committed to a Vision when the Values are not clear and not in line with their personal Value.

# Morning Three Trust

It was a beautiful morning, warm, sunny and perfect for sipping coffee on the patio. It had been a couple of weeks since my last visit with Jean. I was having a little problem with one of my department heads and was hoping to run my ideas past her. So I made a pot of coffee and walked over to Jean's Garden.

Jenkins was lying in the sun on Jean's patio. "Good morning Jenkins. Have we beaten Jean to the Garden?" I asked.

"Not on your life! I've been up for hours." Jean stood up. She had been weeding around the evergreen trees where I could not see her.

"Good morning! Care for a cup of coffee? I'm buying." I offered.

Jean took off her gardening gloves and was wiping her hands on her pants. "How are things going at work?" Jean asked as she walked over to the patio.

"Well as long as you asked, I do have one individual that worries me - Peter. I can't put my finger on it but things are not working smoothly within his department."

"What is he doing?" Jean asked.

"Well, that's just it. It is not any one thing. He says he is on board but the people in his department are not cooperating with the rest of the organization."

Jean responded with a "hmm".

"You sound like a doctor about to deliver bad news," I said.

"It sounds like a trust issue, John. That is a pass – fail situation. If this guy is saying one thing and doing another, there is no commitment and you had better fire him now."

I was stunned. That was not what I was expecting to hear. "I can't do that. Who would run that department? We are very busy. I can't do without him. Besides he is very talented and well respected in the industry."

"No one in the organization is that important, including you." Jean peered over her glasses at me. "If you can't trust your employees but you do nothing about it, then you deserve to lose your company."

I did not respond. Jenkins had hopped over and took up residence under Jean's chair. "John, I don't mean to upset you. I am concerned about you and your organization."

"What makes you so sure that the only way to handle this is termination?"

"Because," began Jean, "a manager who says one thing but does another is creating a culture of mistrust. People in that situation would rather do nothing than risk being blamed or ridiculed for trying to do something. When people do not trust each other, they become defensive. They will avoid working with people they do not trust. It is very hard for an organization to move forward when there is a lack of trust."

"But who will run that department?" I lamented. "I'm barley keeping ahead of things as it is."

"A lack of trust costs the individuals and the organization respect, confidence and ultimately efficiency. If this behavior is not addressed, people will lose trust in you and the Vision," answered Jean. "Leaving Peter in that position is more damaging to your organization than having no one to run the department. Terminating Peter tells everyone in the organization that trust is valued and expected."

"How can you be so sure?" I asked.

Jean responded, "Not all stories have a happy ending."

# *Too Far from the Woodpile*

I would like to introduce you to some of the other creatures that call the Garden home. You may have noticed the white, Victorian bird feeder in the middle of the Garden. It is filled with the most delectable seed. Birds fly in from miles around to dine at this bird feeder.

Birds are very finicky eaters. Seeds they do not like end up on the ground, which is very fortunate for me and my friends. The seeds spring up into tender little plants called sprouts. We love sprouts! That is our favorite breakfast. Come to think of it, it is also our favorite lunch, dinner, and bed time snack, which brings me to my friends.

Every morning we gather for breakfast under the bird feeder. Jean joins us with her cup of coffee, much like you have done today. I am an early riser, so I am usually the first one under the feeder.

Chocolate Longtail scurries along shortly after. He is a nervous little black mouse who takes the most roundabout way of getting to the feeder. He runs along the house under the cover of bushes until he reaches the woodpile near the bird feeder. He never strays too far from the woodpile.

I guess I might be a little skittish, too, if I were as small as he is. Chocolate Longtail is one of those unfortunate creatures whose name is longer than he is, so we call him "Chip" for short. The longest part of Chip is his tail. I have often admired his tail. It is twice as long as the rest of him; pink, in contrast with his black body; and nicely coordinates with his pink nose.

Last to join us are Bip-n-Bop. Bip-n-Bop are mischievous little chipmunks who are always late and will entertain you endlessly with stories of their adventures. There are two of them, twins, with one name, Bip-n-Bop. When we met, they introduced themselves as Bip-n-Bop but never bothered to indicate which was Bip and which was Bop. So I never know which I am talking to. They look so much alike, are always together, and finish each other's sentences; so, they are Bip-n-Bop.

Bip-n-Bop love a good practical joke. They know I am afraid of dogs. Dogs are so loud and have big sharp teeth. For some reason dogs just love to chase me. I'm usually faster than they are and have been able to outrun them, so far. But I would rather avoid the whole scene whenever possible.

Back to the practical joke. There is a statue of a dog in the Garden. I know it is a statue, but it is so life-like that I simply prefer to get past it as quickly as possible. One day I was taking my usual route to the bird feeder, passing a safe distance from the statue. I was almost past it when something caught my eye. I stepped back to get a better look. That statue had grown real fur on its head.

I stood there frozen, which is what I do when I sense danger. After a moment, I heard giggling. I looked up slowly. The hair on the dog popped up.

Bip, or Bop, was perched on that dog's head, looking like a very bad wig. Bip-n-Bop rolled on the ground, laughing and pointing at me. I was just relieved that the dog was still a statue. We had a good laugh over that for days.

One foggy, rainy morning I was not the first to the feeder. "Jenkins, I am so worried. Bop did not return to the burrow last night. I have been searching for hours. Can you help me?" For the first time, I knew which one of Bip-n-Bop I was talking to—but only because Bop was missing.

Just then, from on top of the house we heard, "Who? Who?" What a time for Einstein to show up. Einstein is a very old owl who does not seem to know her own name. We call her Einstein because she appears to be confused and not very bright.

"Bip, you can't find Bop? Where have you looked?" I asked.

"Who? Who?" Einstein interrupted again.

Bip looked so forlorn. "I have looked in all the neighboring gardens."

"Who? Who?" Einstein was persistent.

From under the woodpile we heard, "this is bad, not good." Einstein had obviously made Chip very nervous. "Oh my, oh my."

"Who? Who?" Einstein repeated impatiently.

"Oh, don't worry," I tried to reassure Chip. "I don't think Einstein knows that she is an owl and that she should find little black mice delectable." Then I explained, "Bop is missing."

"What?" Out popped Chip, a little relieved, but still leery. "This is bad. Very, very bad!"

**"Who? Who?"** Einstein firmly demanded, and Chip was back in the woodpile before the second "Who?"

"Bop!" I yelled up to Einstein. "Bop is missing!" I yelled at the top of my lungs. I should not have lost my patience, but I was worried.

"Oh, Oh," said Einstein as she flew down to the feeder.

Chip flattened himself beneath a log. I was very surprised, as Einstein never came to the bird feeder. "I'm sorry," said Einstein. "I've never caught your names. I am a little hard of hearing."

Well, you could have knocked me over with a feather. All this time Einstein was just trying to get to know us. We must have seemed very rude. "I am so sorry. I'm Jenkins. This is Bip and the voice under the woodpile is Chip."

"Hey!" the voice said, "Don't tell her where I am."

I said, "I am sorry. A friend of ours is missing and we are very worried."

"Who? Who?" Einstein repeated again.

"Bop!" we all said. "A little chipmunk that looks exactly like this one," I said, pointing an ear at Bip.

"Ahh, Ahh," said Einstein. "That might be what I heard when I flew over the street this morning. Come along. I'll show you where." She started to move, and then sensed my hesitation. "You have nothing to fear from me. Black mice give me indigestion."

Off we all went as fast as our little legs could carry us. Einstein was flying, Bip and I were trying to follow, and Chip, not wanting to be left behind, was scurrying under bushes wherever possible.

As we approached the street, I could hear the faint cries of a very scared creature. Einstein landed beside the grate in the street.

Bip and I ran to her side and peered in. There was poor Bop. Wet, cold, and obviously frightened. Bop looked up and began to cry, "I thought I would never be found!"

"How will we get him out of there?" Bip wailed.

"How? How?" asked Einstein. "We need something long and thin to lower down to Bop so he can climb out."

"But what?" I wondered as I looked around for something long and thin.

"Chip." Einstein was way ahead of us. Chip had a long tail. She knew we were going to need it. That is why she had asked Chip to come along. "You are the only one who can help Bop. We need you, Buddy," said Einstein.

"No." Chip was hiding under a bush next to the house. "Not with you standing there."

Einstein nodded. "I will wait at the end of the block. I promise not to harm you. Please help your friend." And with that, Einstein spread her wings and flew to the end of the block.

Chip did not, or could not, move. This was going to take all of his courage. He would have to run from the cover of the bushes, stand exposed in the street, and let Bop climb up his tail. And I wasn't sure that his tail was going to be strong enough.

"Chip, please hurry," pleaded Bip.

Bob responded from inside the grate, "That's okay. We cannot ask Chip to do this."

Upon hearing Bops' sad voice, Chip appeared from under the bushes. With a look of determination I had never seen on a little mouse face, he ran to the grate and exclaimed, "I HOPE THIS WORKS!"

Chip slipped his tail between the grates but his tail was not quite long enough. Bop found some rubbish and piled it as high as he could. He was closer, but still not quite tall enough. Then Bip found a small branch and tossed it down to Bop. With that, Bop was able to just grab hold of Chip's tail.

Chip pulled with all his strength. But Bop weighed too much, and Chip began to slide toward the grate. Bip grabbed hold of Chip. I grabbed hold of Bip. And we all began to pull together until the small mass of brown fur slipped up through the grate. We all fell back with a thud. There we were, lying in a heap— Chip, Bip, and Bop and me.

"Job well done," Einstein called as she flew on her way.

"Thank you. Thank you a thousand times," we yelled and waved. "Please join us for breakfast soon!"

Bop was hugging Chip. "That was very brave of you. Thank you."

"Weren't you afraid?" asked Bip.

Chip looked very thoughtful. "I figured Einstein could have eaten me any time, but she never did. Besides, you guys are worth the risk."

The next morning I was the first one under the feeder, as usual. I was enjoying the peaceful morning, and deep in thought. I did not notice Bip-n-Bop walking up behind me, so when they tapped me on my foot I jumped five yards into the air! When I landed, Bip-n-Bop were rolling around on the ground, holding their tummies and laughing so hard they could not talk.

"Dear me! You scared me half to death!" I replied when I finally quit shaking. "I guess I was so deep in thought I did not hear you coming."

Bip-n-Bop were busily running up the linden tree. "Thinking that hard must hurt," they giggled.

"Well I was just wondering what would have happened if Chip had not helped you or worse, Einstein had eaten Chip," I said.

Bip-n-Bop stopped dead in their tracks. "This would be a very different Garden," they replied. A Garden without trust, no one wanted to even think about it.

# Limit, Assess, Change

The ability to quickly identify, confidently assess and effectively change behavior is a strong leader's greatest asset. Behavior that is assessed and addressed at the moment it is observed makes the biggest impact because it defines assumptions and clarifies expectations. It communicates what is important, what will not be accepted, and that leadership is watching.

## LIMIT THE ISSUES

How often have you left a meeting or discussion thinking, "what did that mean" or "why are they doing that?" The behavior may seem meaningless or just pesky, however when something just doesn't "sit right" a good leader takes the time to find out why. This is the point where most managers ignore behaviors because they feel overwhelmed by all the possibilities. If you are not aware of how people are behaving, you will miss the opportunity to define assumptions, clarify expectations and effect change.

The reason some behaviors do not stand out as damaging is because people are experts at creating situations, excuses and blame to disguise the real issue. The Vision and Values statements limit issues by answering; who are we, what do we do, why do we do it, and how. Determining what the issue is as simple as asking, does this person understand:

- Who we are? (Trust)
- What we do? (Assumptions)
- Why we do it? (Priorities)
- How we do it? (Values)

## ASSESS THE ISSUE

Performance management systems are supposed to provide information about the organization's human capitol. In reality, these systems have been put in place primarily to assess how people performed so that raises and promotions appear to have been awarded equitably. For example, perform an Internet search for "performance management" and note that all kinds of software tools pop up; what are we managing – software or people?

Much like the financial statement, performance data is often gathered annually, quarterly at best, and is based in part on the financial statement and memory. It does not promote performance assessment in real time or assess behaviors and issues that are going to cause problems in the future. It does not allow managers to make confident decisions before results hit the bottom line. In fact, by tying performance assessment to annual reviews, the organization has provided managers an excuse for not confronting performance problems. Because managers are uncomfortable confronting people, they will put off addressing the issue until the assigned time. Assessments that occur annually are too late, too complicated and ineffective. Assessment is part of the good leader's daily routine.

People use excuses and blame to deflect responsibility and rationalize behavior. Managers have many responsibilities and a lot on their plate. Who has time to figure out what people are doing, leave alone why! Therefore assessment must be a simple and visual comparison of issue to vision, a comparison of who the individual is verses who the organization is.

## PERFORMANCE ASSESSMENT

| Org. Vision | Goals the organization wants to achieve | Contributions the organization wants to make | Things the organization wants to help others do | How will the organization be remembered |
|---|---|---|---|---|
| Issues | Who are we?<br><br>*Trust* | What do we do?<br><br>*Assumptions* | Why do we do it?<br><br>*Priorities* | How do we do it?<br><br>*Values* |

## WHO ARE WE? - TRUST

Fear, disrespect, blame and excuses are behaviors that indicate an issue of trust. If you ask this person, "Do you understand who we are?" and they do not answer with the organization's goal, there is an issue of trust.

People who are more committed to themselves than to the organization's goal create confusion. They blame other departments when delivery is late. They say one thing and do another. They will create excuses and blame leadership for setting the wrong goals. Furthermore, they will try to win people to their agenda and create division within the organization. This individual will distort the Vision for their advantage. If this behavior is not stopped, people within the organization will lose trust in leadership. It does not matter what this individual's position or perceived value is. They must not be allowed to stay with the organization.

# Morning Four Priorities

The morning after firing Peter, I made a pot of coffee and took it over to Jean's patio. Jean was not out yet so I poured myself a cup and sat down. It was a beautiful day. The warm sun was baking off the dew. Jenkins was under the bird feeder eating sprouts. Birds were singing. Two little chipmunks came running across the patio and joined Jenkins under the feeder. That was when I noticed a little black mouse sitting on the wood pile.

It had been three weeks since I last spoke with Jean. I did not fire Peter right after our last meeting. In fact, I had no intention of firing Peter - until yesterday.

"Good morning John! I am glad to see you." Jean was coming out of her house. She seemed surprised to see me. "After our last meeting I was not sure I would ever see you again."

"I'm sorry, Jean. I just could not imagine firing Peter. It seemed like such a drastic move. I thought you might be interested to know - I fired Peter yesterday."

"Wow! How was that received?" Jean sat down and held her cup out for me to pour the coffee.

"It was amazing. It was as if the whole organization took a deep breath. Most people were happy, said it was about time." I poured Jean a cup of coffee. "Thank you."

Jean took a sip. "You said most people. I'm sure there is a lot of talk going on. Are you sure everyone understands why you fired Peter when you did?" I must have looked confused because Jean went on. "There will be all kinds of interpretations of what went on and why you fired Peter now."

"I'm not sure I understand. No one liked working with this guy. What's to explain?"

"As far as everyone else is concerned, Peter has been difficult for a long time. Why was he fired now?" Jean asked.

I explained to Jean that I happened upon Peter and one of his direct reports in the hall. Peter was yelling at this person, telling him he had no business going directly to the Director of Quality. I couldn't believe my ears and I immediately thought of Chip. I walked up to Peter and fired him right there in front of his direct report.

"Well done!" Jean shook my hand. "Just remember, when someone is fired, all kinds of rumors will start. People might be happy he's gone, but they were under the assumption that he was well respected in the industry and important to the organization. People might jump to the conclusion that the company is in financial trouble and be worried that they might be next."

"Well that's just ridiculous," I said.

"From where you're sitting, that may be, but put yourself in the employees' shoes," said Jean. "After all, Peter had been with the company for quite a while. As far as everyone else is concerned, Peter had always mistreated others. Why was he fired now?"

"Because…" I started.

Jean interrupted. "What you choose to communicate and when you communicate it informs everyone what your priorities are. Every decision you make, action you take or do not take, will be interpreted. Remember," she said, "your behavior communicates what is important to you. Peter's behavior had not been addressed for a long time. Behaviors that you choose not to address will be perceived as unimportant – so why now?"

"Because he was misstreating that employee," I responded.

"Remember John, the person talking the most will be defining the Vision. This is your opportunity to define your Vision and Values. When people are blaming each other, creating excuses, and speculating on the cause of the problem, it can be very difficult to determine the real issue."

"Now I remember why I stayed out of the people part of my business," I groaned.

Jean smiled. "It can become a tangled web with no way out unless you remember: it is not your job to figure out **why** people are behaving in a particular way. It is your responsibility to assess **how** their behavior affects the organization."

"Peter's behavior had reached a point it was negatively affecting the organization," I said.

"How?" asked Jean.

I was thinking Jean was sounding a lot like Einstein when she said, "What the organization helps others do defines priorities. The Garden helps creatures live peacefully. If what I am doing is not helping creatures who want to live peacefully, then I do not value the Vision. Fortunately, or unfortunately, communication occurs with each decision leadership makes, in every meeting, and every encounter. When leadership ignores certain behaviors or allows particular individuals to behave differently, then priorities have changed. The focus is no longer on the Vision. What does your organization help others do?"

"We help our customers deliver safe, effective drugs," I answered.

"And how does your organization do that?" Jean asked.

"We deliver quality product," I answered.

"How was Peter's behavior affecting the organization's ability to deliver quality product to your customer?'

"His behavior threatened the quality of our product.

"So, you didn't fire him because he was yelling at an employee. You fired him because he was not committed to your Vision." Jean smiled. "A well timed question can make all the difference. In fact, I just observed something very similar in the Garden."

# Acorn Lesson

Did you happen to notice the bump on my head? There were so many misunderstandings in the Garden this week. I am embarrassed to admit that I was part of the problem. Needless to say, we had to get our priorities in order.

It was a bright, crisp, fall day earlier this week. The birds were chirping and eating in the bird feeder. Chip and I were enjoying some fresh young sprouts. It was a peaceful, beautiful morning in the Garden. Suddenly Bip-n-Bop tore across the lawn as fast as I had ever seen their little legs move. And, of course, they were babbling to each other.

"Bip, are you all right? I'll be alright. How are you? Well, I'll live, no thanks to Earl and his buddies. Someone should have a talk with them. I should say so. What do you think that was all about?" Bip-n-Bop were out of breath, but that did not hinder their incessant chattering.

Chip looked at me with his "here-we-go-again" expression. I thumped my foot rather loudly to get their attention. "What has the two of you so upset?"

"Earl and his buddies!" they exclaimed.

There is a tall, stately oak tree in the neighboring garden. Some of its branches hang over into the Garden. This tree is home to Earl Squirrel and his squirrel buddies. "What are the Squirrels up to now?" I asked.

"They threw acorns at us! They nearly hit Bop. Acorns were raining down on us. We could have been injured, or worse. I thought they liked us. I like them. Well, I do too - or did...."

Bip-n-Bop chattered on and on to each other and had forgotten that Chip and I were there. Chip shook his head and wandered back to the woodpile for his early morning nap.

I tried to reassure them. "Look, there are some delicious young sprouts over here. Very tasty." Fortunately Bip-n-Bop are easily distracted and began nibbling on the sprouts.

Later that afternoon, Chip woke from his nap and wandered out to the Black-Eyed Susan, where I had found a warm spot to rest. "What were Bip-n-Bop carrying on about this morning?" he yawned.

I still was not sure so I said, "Would you care to walk with me to the oak tree and have a chat with Earl?"

As we approached the oak tree, Chip and I heard loud barking and growling. We hid under a bush. A large dog jumped and snarled at the base of the tree. The dog was so big that he could jump half way up the tree. The poor squirrels were huddled together as high in the tree as they could get. The dog looked vicious. His lips curled up, making his teeth appear even longer and sharper. His growl was ominous. This was a very angry creature. Chip whispered, "Now I see why you are so afraid of dogs."

I could not speak. Nothing scares me more than dogs – all dogs, but this dog was especially scary. Eventually, the dog tired and wandered on down the street. No one moved for several minutes.

Earl was the first to crawl cautiously down the trunk of the tree. Chip and I peeked out from under the bush. "That was scary!" exclaimed Chip.

"Yes, it was. Unusually so," responded Earl. "I wish I understood why dogs dislike us so."

I finally found my voice. "I have never understood why dogs enjoy scaring rabbits and squirrels. I'm usually hopping away so fast that I do not think to ask them why they are chasing me." We all laughed nervously.

"Well, my buddies and I decided to teach those dogs a lesson," proclaimed Earl.

# ACORN LESSON

I could not fathom how anyone could possibly teach a dog anything. "Really?" I asked. "How are you doing that?"

"We drop acorns on them." Earl was clearly proud of his plan.

"How does that work?" I found the idea of teaching dogs a lesson very enticing.

"Here comes another dog," warned Earl. "Hide and watch this."

Earl and his buddies ran back up the tree. A young woman walking a dog strolled into the Garden. When an acorn suddenly fell from the tree and hit the dog on the head, he was obviously very confused. The dog looked high and low, but could not figure out what had hit him. The woman put her arm up to protect her own head and pulled the dog away from the Garden. There was no barking. There was no jumping. It was a miracle!

"Marvelous!" I exclaimed, "Oh, how exciting! I wish I could climb trees and drop acorns on dogs."

Chip seemed less impressed. He tugged at my fur, begging me to leave. He said he needed to get back to his woodpile–something about a nap.

"Way to go! I'll see you tomorrow." I waved an ear to Earl and the Squirrels.

"Chip, did you see that?" I was so excited. "It was so simple. And the dog was so confused. Actually, it was rather funny, don't you think? That dog probably thought the sky was falling. He could not figure out what hit him or where it came from. Most importantly, he was quiet! There was no barking or chasing. An absolutely stunning, brilliant idea....." I could not stop talking about the dog and the acorns.

Chip interrupted, "I have a bad feeling about this."

The next few mornings I was up early. I could not wait to get back to the oak tree. I ate breakfast quickly before Chip and Bip-n-Bop were even awake. It was so much fun watching the squirrels drop acorns on dogs. I was absolutely obsessed with watching them.

One day, Chip appeared suddenly. "I had a feeling this was where I would find you," he said when he found me.

"Hello, Chip. Were you looking for me? Watch this. I have made up a cheer. Point an ear to the left and say, 'Drop from the left'. Then point an ear to the right and say, 'Drop from the right'. Then hop and yell ACORNS, ACORNS…."

Chip interrupted me with a frown, "I think you might be enjoying this just a little too much."

I was offended. "Chip, why did you come looking for me?"

"We all miss you. Bip-n-Bop, the Robins, Einstein. They have been asking about you," replied Chip.

"I have simply been watching the squirrels teach the dogs a lesson," I retorted.

Just then, a dog wondered into the Garden, and acorns began to fly from every direction. Earl and his buddies were serious. But before Chip and I could retreat beneath the bush, an acorn hit me on the head - hard.

"Owwww!" I yelled.

Earl scurried quickly down from the tree. "Jenkins, are you all right? I am so sorry. We did not mean to hit you. Please forgive us."

Chip climbed on top of my head to inspect the bump. "I knew nothing good would come of this."

Earl stopped short. "What's that you say, Chip?"

Chip looked embarrassed. "I just mean, what is the lesson you are trying to teach the dogs?"

"Oh, my." Earl looked as though a dozen acorns had assailed his head. "Have we become the problem?" He asked.

So, you see, I am very glad you came to the Garden today. We have our priorities in order now.

# What to Measure

Once the issue has been identified, there is only one thing to measure – commitment. Every person's behavior must communicate a commitment to the Vision. People who are committed to the organization will take responsibility beyond their job description. They make choices, take action, and deliver more than what is expected. People who are committed to themselves will, at best, only be responsible for their job. The choices they make will result in late delivery or delivery of the wrong thing.

| ORGANIZATION | COMMITMENT | INDIVIDUAL |
|---|---|---|
| Who we are | Goals | Who the person is |
| What we do | Assumptions | What the person does |
| Who we do it for | Priorities | Who the person does it for |
| How we do it | Values | How the person does it |

It is for this reason that job descriptions should be written with individual contributions and not responsibilities. If everyone is responsible for the organization's goals, the question becomes, what does each person contribute? People who contribute more than their job description are very committed to the organization. People who contribute just enough to meet their job requirements are borderline committed. They will stay late - if it fits into their schedule. They will double check their work - if they feel like it. People, who refuse to make the contributions needed to get their job done, and done right, are not committed to the organization at all.

## *Job Descriptions*

Ask an individual what they contribute to the organization and you may discover that they do not know who or what they are responsible for. For this reason, job descriptions should focus on contributions rather than responsibilities.

Responsibilities build excuses into the system and provide individuals with the opportunity to say, "That isn't my job. My responsibility was to do ___. I did my part." People are more likely to take responsibility when they understand the importance of their contribution to the organization's goals.

Contributions to the organization, defines individual priorities. When an individual does not understand what to do or why they are doing it, they will deliver the wrong thing at the wrong time and blame other people.

Job descriptions become tools for communicating the organization's Vision to every individual in the organization. Relating departmental and individual Visions to the organization's Vision creates a single message, continuity and a standard against which performance can be measured.

## PERFORMANCE ASSESSMENT

Performance assessment must measure commitment against expectations and relate it to a specific behavior or event. There are three levels of commitment and four expectations:

## WHAT TO MEASURE

## LEVELS OF COMMITMENT

1. To the organization
2. To the job description
3. To the individual

## EXPECTATION

1. Who we are
2. What we do
3. Why we do it
4. How we do it

Ambiguity and subjectivity are removed from the assessment process when levels of commitment and performance issues are limited. There are no percentages. Real numbers are generated and substantiated by specific behaviors and observations.

The performance assessment form below creates a visual representation that clearly lays out where the performance problems are and provides an opportunity to coach and identify specific actions that can be taken to improve. Placing an "X" at the organization level under the trust performance issue and relating a specific instance when they exhibited an

understanding of the organization's goals is much more specific than saying this individual met 60% of their goals.

## PERFORMANCE ASSESSMENT FORM

| Vision | Organization Goals | Contributions We Make | What We Help Others Do | Qualities For Which We Want to be Remembered |
|---|---|---|---|---|
| **Expectations** | Who We Are | What We Do | Why We Do It | How We Do It |
| **Performance Issues** | **Trust** | **Assumptions** | **Priorities** | **Values** |
| **Organization** | | | | |
| | **Job Description** | | | |
| **Individual Vision and Values** | | | | |

(Commitment arrow spans from Organization down to Individual Vision and Values)

Different situations and events will confuse and cloud what is really going on. It is for this reason the issues must be limited to; trust, assumptions, priorities, and Values. Take for example the person who is a great planner. They can see how the department could run better. They devise a great plan – but the plan is not implemented. To assess what the issue might be, ask yourself:

## Does this person understand who the organization is?

Yes. They devised a great plan that the organization will benefit from. They could not have devised such a plan if they did not understand who the company is. Then trust is not the issue.

## Does this person know what we do?

The plan fits right in with what we do. It would be a great asset. Then assumption is not the issue.

## Does this person understand why we do it?

The question "what do we help others do?" is used when developing the Vision to define priorities. The answer to that question defines who will reap the benefit from our doing our jobs well. When people loose sight of who the organization does it for, they will deliver the wrong thing and then they will blame the person they were suppose to be doing it for.

If you ask; "Does this person understand why we do it?" and the answer is no, there must be a priorities issue. Is there something else that they are doing that they think is more important? Is there something that they need to get the job done?

Now you have something to coach and a language that will make your coaching more effective. For example:

*"I really liked your improvement plan for the department. I was hoping that it would be a priority for you. What have you done to get it implemented? Is there anything you need to get this accomplished? When will it be completed?"*

If, after some coaching, the plan is still not implemented, you have a trust issue. They are not committed to delivering what the organization needs. If they were, they would overcome their personal issue and deliver. It does not matter why this person is ineffective. For all you know their mother may have slapped their hand every time they tried to help. This is not to say that the organization should not help this individual overcome their issue. However, over time they will feel they need to redeem themselves in the eyes of their coworkers. They will start blaming others and create dissent. Remember you are in business. You are not a physiatrist. *Your* first priority is to the organization's goal.

# Morning Five Assumptions

Jean had been helping my wife with our yard. In fact, our yard was beginning to look like a garden. So before going to work, I took my cup of coffee out to the patio. I slid the door open and stepped outside where I discovered Jenkins under our patio table.

"Good morning Jenkins. Keeping the rabbits out of our Garden, I hope? Is Jean out yet?" I was wandering over to Jean's patio when Jean stepped out from her house, coffee cup in hand.

"Good morning John! I see you and Jenkins have become good friends," Jean laughed.

I hadn't noticed that Jenkins was following me. I rolled my eyes and shook my head. "I'm not sure I'd say good friends. Do you have a little time? I have something I want to run past you."

"Sure, John, what's up?"

Well, I am a little frustrated with my Director of Quality."

"Really?" asked Jean. "You have always spoken so highly of her."

It was true. Lisa, the Director of Quality, was one of my best employees. I had great respect for her knowledge. "Don't get me wrong," I said. "Lisa is probably one of the best hires I've ever made…"

"But?" Jean asked.

"She's not enforcing our quality procedures."

Jean looked puzzled and said, "If I remember correctly, Lisa established the quality department."

"Yes. She wrote all of our quality operating procedures and trained everyone across all departments. That's what makes this so difficult," I said. "It's not like she doesn't know what the procedures are."

"Have you talked with her about this issue?" Jean asked.

"That's the interesting part, she brought it up."

Jean looked surprised. "How so?"

I explained that Lisa came to me very frustrated because she had done all this training and people were still not adhering to the procedures.

Jean sat back in her chair and asked me, "When you hired Lisa, what did you need her to do?"

"I needed someone who knew the quality standards for the industry and could improve our quality department."

"Sounds like she did her job," replied Jean.

"Well not really. If she does not enforce the procedures, there is no quality. You're the one who said when behaviors are not addressed, they become standard operating procedure," I reminded Jean.

"That is true," smiled Jean. "But you're assuming Lisa understands that enforcing the procedures is part of her job."

"Well if it isn't her job, whose job is it?" I asked.

"John, Lisa is frustrated for the same reason you are. You're assuming that she understands that it is her responsibility to enforce the procedures. Lisa is assuming that everyone understands the procedures and should therefore be following them."

I was still thinking about what Jean just said when she went on, "Assumption issues cause frustration and blame. No one can succeed if they are working on the wrong problem."

"So Lisa is working on the wrong problem?" I asked.

"Well, let's look at the behavior," said Jean. "You said Lisa is frustrated. Who is she blaming for the lack of adherence to the procedures?"

"She is blaming everyone else," I answered.

"Why are you frustrated, John?"

"Well that's obvious," I said. "Because people are not following the quality procedures and we are not delivering quality product to our customers."

"And who do you blame for that?" asked Jean.

"Lisa," I answered.

"Well at least you and Lisa agree on something," laughed Jean.

"Yeah, people are not following the quality procedures!" I smiled.

"That, and delivering quality product is important," said Jean. "Lisa is committed to the Vision, John. It's just her assumptions are incorrect – and so are yours. This is a great coaching opportunity, John."

"You mean she doesn't know it's her responsibility to enforce the procedures?" I asked.

"Not only that," said Jean. "She doesn't know how."

I looked at Jenkins who was lying under the bird feeder and said, "I feel a story coming on."

Jean looked over her reading glasses and smiled.

# *A Most Wonderful Day*

This happened one hot day last week. Oh, I wish you could have been here. Bip-n-Bop were so busy running all about making sure everything was perfect. Chip nearly lost his beautiful long tail when the woodpile fell. And Mr. and Mrs. C.— Forgive me; you don't know Mr. and Mrs. C. yet. I really should start at the beginning.

Mr. and Mrs. C. are a pair of cardinals. They are the most beautiful couple to visit the Garden. Mr. C. is bright red with a stunning black face and yellow beak. His head is crowned with a luxurious comb of red feathers. Mrs. C.'s feathers are subtle blend of the many shades of red, yellow, and orange. They are a striking pair. And gifted. They possess the most beautiful singing voices. Their song is very distinctive and melodious. We hear them long before they arrive in the Garden. Then we enjoy them as they sit high in the trees and sing to each other.

No other couple in the Garden is as happy as Mr. and Mrs. C. They are always so polite and courteous to each other. Mr. C. waits for Mrs. C. to eat first as he watches her adoringly. Then Mrs. C. watches as Mr. C. eats and serenades him from the highest branch of the tallest tree in the Garden.

Every day since Jean put the bird feeder up, Mr. and Mrs. C. have come to eat at the feeder and serenade each other. All the creatures in the Garden stop to watch and admire this elegant couple, and we feel honored to be in their presence and enjoy their beautiful music.

One day, I was enjoying fresh sprouts under the feeder, listening to Mrs. C.'s delightful song as Mr. C. ate from the feeder.

# MORNINGS WITH JENKINS

Suddenly, birdseed began to hit my ears and I heard, "Hey! Hey! Jenkins, Jenkins Rabbit." I looked around for Bip-n-Bop or Chip or Einstein. But I didn't see anyone. Then I heard, "Jenkins, look up."

"My dear, Mr. C.," I said. "I am sorry. I don't mean to be rude. I was just enjoying your wife's song and my sprouts so thoroughly..."

"Yes, yes", interrupted Mr. C. rather impatiently. "I haven't much time, and I need some help."

"Well, I would be happy to do whatever I can," I responded. I could not imagine what kind of problem Mr. C. could possibly have, or how I could possibly help.

"Mrs. C and I will be celebrating our anniversary next week and I have no idea what to get her."

"I can see where that would be a problem..." I began.

"Dear me," Mr. C. interrupted again, "I must go now. Mrs. C. is getting impatient. Please give this some thought, if you wouldn't mind. I'll be back tomorrow." And with that, Mr. and Mrs. C. flew away side by side.

Mr. and Mrs. C. seem to be so happy. They seem to have everything. But I saw how that could be a problem. What do you give someone who seems to have everything?

I looked around and, of course, Bip-n-Bop were nowhere to be found. Chip was asleep in the woodpile. And Einstein, even if she could be found, would just ask, "Who? Who?" For most of the evening, I pondered Mr. C's dilemma. I was unable to sleep and getting worried. What was I going to say to Mr. C.? I did not want to let him down.

In the morning I went looking for someone—anyone—to help me. But this appeared to be the morning that everyone chose to sleep in. Doesn't that figure? When you want some peace and quiet, you can't get creatures to leave you alone. And when you want to talk, you can't find a soul.

Then my search was cut short by the beautiful song that I usually enjoyed so much. Mr. and Mrs. C. were coming. The song grew louder. They were getting closer. Quickly.

What was I going to say? I did not have a single suggestion for Mr. C. "Excuse me!" I looked up to see Mrs. C. descending on the feeder. "Excuse me, Jenkins! I do hate to trouble you, but I could use your help."

"I would be happy to help however I can," I replied.

"Mr. C. and I have an anniversary next week," she looked around and lowered her melodic voice, "and I cannot think of a thing to give him. Has he said anything to you?"

"Well, as a matter of fact," I answered, "Mr. C is having the same problem. He cannot think of a thing to get you. Maybe you two should just talk to each other." I thought, There, I fixed their problem and I will be able to get a good night's sleep tonight.

"We would, but we can't," Mrs. C. replied. "We cannot ever sit together."

"What?" I exclaimed. This seemed unreasonable. Why couldn't two birds so obviously in love sit together?

"Our colors are so bright that we are easily spotted by creatures that could hurt us. We take turns keeping watch while the other eats. We sing while we keep watch to assure each other that we are safe," explained Mrs. C.

"Dear me, I thought you were just being courteous to each other." I had never noticed that Mr. and Mrs. C. never ate together.

"Mr. C. is anxious to go," Mrs. C. exclaimed. "I will be back tomorrow. I would appreciate any assistance you can provide." And they flew away.

Just then Bip-n-Bop came running across the Garden. They, of course, could not simply run straight across the garden. They were playing tag, somersaulting over each other and giggling hysterically. In their oblivious giddiness, they tripped over each other and rolled right into me. They lay in a heap, holding their sides, laughing so hard they could not even talk.

Chip poked his head out of the woodpile, obviously angry that his nap had been interrupted. "What is all the racket?" Chip was very cross.

# MORNINGS WITH JENKINS

"Just the usual shenanigans," I replied. "But I am very glad you are all here. I have a problem that I hope you can assist me with."

"Oh dear. Oh my. A problem? What could it be? Do you think we can help? Do you think we should help? What kind of problem could Jenkins have? Do you think he was talking to us? Who? What?"

In the chaos, no one had any idea who said what. Bip-n-Bop have a way of finishing each other's thoughts and never arriving at a conclusion.

Chip was fully awake now and looked quite concerned. "Jenkins, you know you can count on me!"

"I know I can count on all of you," I said. Then, I explained Mr. and Mrs. C.'s predicament.

"Who would have thought? How can this be? I never would have guessed! Did that ever occur to you? I don't know how we could help. How does this possibly affect us?" Bip-n-Bop ran up the linden tree, continuing their game of tag and not waiting for any answers.

Chip and I just thought for a while in silence. Then it hit me, "I know! We are going to throw them a party."

"A party? Oh hurray! I do love a good party. When is it? Who shall we invite? What shall I wear? You only have the one outfit! Oh, I know, but I get so tired of wearing the same old thing." Bip-n-Bop came running back down the tree.

Chip was sitting on top of the woodpile. "How is a party going to help Mr. and Mrs. C.?"

"Who, Who?" By now, Einstein had also arrived.

"Mr. and Mrs. C.," I answered. "So glad you could join us, Einstein. I am going to need your help. I need you to invite every bird you know to join us in the Garden tomorrow. Bip-n-Bop, I need you to decorate the bird feeder. Chip, I need you to gather all the seed you can find."

# A MOST WONDERFUL DAY

Everyone scurried away busily, and by the next afternoon they were ready. I had never seen the feeder so beautiful. Bip-n-Bop lined the roof with flowers. The feeder overflowed with seed. Every tree and rooftop were full of birds.

I sat, waiting in the middle of the Garden. When Mr. and Mrs. C. finally flew into the topmost branch of the aspen tree, I called, "Mr. and Mrs. C.!"

"Yes, Jenkins?" they replied in unison.

"Happy anniversary!" all the animals cried together.

"What?" Mr. and Mrs. C. were very surprised.

"Welcome to your anniversary party!" I announced. "We are all here to be your lookouts while you two eat from the feeder together. This is our anniversary gift to you."

From the rooftops and trees began the most beautiful chorus nature had ever heard. Einstein escorted Mr. and Mrs. C. to the feeder, where they dined together for the first time ever.

Bip-n-Bop were so pleased that they hopped and clapped on top of the woodpile. Chip watched safely from under the woodpile, his smile almost as long as his tail. Suddenly, the pile of wood began to collapse. Chip darted, trying to get out of the way, but his beautiful tail was caught between two logs. Bip-n-Bop ran to the rescue and pulled Chip to safety.

We all sighed in relief when we saw Bip-n-Bop and Chip rolling and laughing on the ground.

Mr. and Mrs. C. sang a beautiful song for us from on top of the feeder. "Thank you, thank you and thank you, all! What a wonderful day this has been!" they exclaimed.

Wonderful indeed! We all learned a lot about each other that week. Most importantly, things are not always as they appear.

# How to Communicate

Today's predominate management belief is given enough resources, people will get the job done. If goals are defined and people are encouraged to provide input, treated with honor and respect, people will be held accountable and produce. The problem with this model is that performance is being assessed based on goals that were established during last year's assessment. In today's business environment, many goals are obsolete in a week, never mind a year. Furthermore, leadership has taken all the responsibility for setting goals, providing the tools, resources and encouragement. The employees have been given an excuse for not delivering. In the employees' mind they are not responsible if goals are not met. Leadership set the goals. If tools break down, customer needs change, or it's vacation time - the employee is not accountable. Management is responsible. On the flip side, if management continually changes the goals to meet the ever-changing business environment, management is perceived as indecisive.

This is when the vision becomes the strategic plan. The strategic plan lays out what needs to be done, how it will be done, who will do it and, assesses progress toward reaching the long range goal. There are four phases to strategic planning; formulation, development, implementation, and evaluation. Each phase correlates with a stage of development, the organization's vision and every individual within the organization.

## THE PLAN IS THE PROCESS

The strategic plan becomes a dynamic and continuous process. Despite the strict and sequential look of the figure below, the process is not as cleanly divided and neatly implemented in real life. An adaption in any part of the model can necessitate a change in any or all of the other phases. Every phase of the plan must be reevaluated, planned for, implemented, and communicated everyday – to every employee – all year long.

### STRATEGIC PLANNING PROCESS

| Phase I | Phase II | Phase III | Phase IV |
|---|---|---|---|
| Strategy Formulation | Strategy Development | Strategy Implementation | Strategy Evaluation |
| Vision Long Range Goal | Mission This Year's Plan for Reaching the Long Range Goal | Responsibilities Department Individual | Performance Assessment |
| Who We Are | What We Do | Why We Do It | How We Do It |

## MANAGE THE PLAN – LEAD PEOPLE

When a manager's focus becomes creating, continually assessing, and communicating the plan they become leaders. Furthermore, when everyone knows who they are, what they are doing, why they are doing it and how they are performing any change to the plan will be easier to implement.

## TOOLS FOR COMMUNICATING

There are only two issues that can be coached: assumptions and priorities. Assessing and coaching behavior at the moment it is observed provides managers an opportunity to clarify assumptions and define priorities. However, to be effective you must have a clear understanding of what and how to assess and coach.

The Garden's Vision is to provide a safe home for all creatures willing to contribute to the peace and safety of the Garden. It does not matter if your position is robin, rabbit or chipmunk. You are responsible for peace and safety in the Garden. The same is true in a business. The goal for most businesses is to make money. Each individual must be committed to that goal. Accountability occurs when people understand the importance of what the organization does and what each individual contributes to that goal. Individuals will confidently take action and responsibility when they believe in the big picture and understand the importance and impact they have on the Vision.

Take, for example, a project management department lead by a manager who routinely makes decisions and takes action on individual projects without consulting the project leader. The department manager takes a vacation and, because he was not aware of the reasons for previous decisions made by the manager, the project leader makes a decision that results in late delivery, reduced profit for that project, and an unhappy customer.

The department manager assumes that he is responsible for all projects. The project leader also rightly assumes that he was responsible for the project he was assigned. This is not a situation where no one is taking responsibility. This is an issue of assumptions.

The job description for the Head of Project Management might read:

> *The Head of Project Management contributes to the organization's success by ensuring all projects meet or exceed quality standards and are delivered at or below budget.*

How is the manager expected to do that? What should the manager contribute and to whom? If the manager answers, "Delivering quality projects on time," the manager is working from the assumption that his priority is the projects when, in reality, his priority should be the project leaders. When an individual becomes a manager, their priorities change. Their focus becomes broader. In the case of the manager, he is no longer responsible for a project. He is responsible for assisting the individuals who are responsible for projects. Coaching the manager when he is making decisions without the project leader provides the manager an opportunity to correct his behavior and increase his value. If these assumptions are not clarified, expectations will not be realized.

# HOW

Some behaviors increase an individual's value to the organization. Some behaviors decrease an individual's value. Every person thinks they are valuable. Where a job is on the pay scale is one way to determine a person's worth. But for an individual to truly understand the expectations of their job, behaviors that result in direct and indirect costs must be identified.

It is fairly easy to indentify behaviors that result in direct costs to the organization. The cost of late delivery or the loss of a customer is easily identified. The behaviors that are not as easily observed and identifiable can be much more costly to the organization and the individual. The respect lost and the damage done to the organization's Vision and Values can bring a leader and the organization down if not addressed.

Behavior costs that reduce an individual's value to the organization must be described. The manager must be told that when project leaders are not included in the decision making process, people within the department loose trust in management. To be successful in his job, his priority must be the project leaders. Including project leaders in the quoting process, coaching them, assisting in scheduling and providing them the tools needed to successfully manage their projects will result in his department's ability to produce more profitable, quality projects. If his priorities are not redirected, he will be unable to increase capacity and he will not be contributing to the organizations profitability. More importantly, if this behavior is allowed to continue, the Vision will have been redefined and people will loose trust in leadership and the organization.

# Morning Six Leadership

I had not seen Jean for several weeks. Work was keeping me busy, but I was enjoying it more. I was going to work with a renewed energy, looking for opportunities to communicate my Vision and regaining control of my company. It was a beautiful fall morning so I made a pot of coffee and went over to Jean's patio hoping that she would be there too.

When I arrived, Jenkins was sunning himself on the patio. Two chipmunks were eating sprouts under the bird feeder. I poured myself a cup of coffee and noticed a little black mouse peering at me from under the wood pile.

"Well, I see that nothing has changed. Nice to see you, Jenkins." I was having a pleasant conversation with Jenkins and was just about to ask if he had seen Jean yet this morning, when Jean emerged from her house, coffee cup in hand. "John! What a pleasant surprise. I've missed our morning chats. How are you?"

We hugged and I offered Jean a cup of coffee. "I just wanted to stop by and tell you what a difference our conversations have made in my company. In fact, my wife and I are going to take a two week vacation."

"Congratulations, John!" Jean held her cup up and said, "To John and his Vision! I am so happy for you."

"It truly is a pleasure going to work. People are stepping up, taking responsibility and getting the job done. Even people that I didn't have much confidence in are taking action and are making terrific decisions."

"That reminds me. How is your quality manager doing?" Asked Jean

"Much better," I said. "But it took a few conversations before I figured out what questions I needed to be asking and to understand how to coach her."

"When did you figure that out?" Jean asked.

"Well, Lisa would come in every once in a while with one issue or another. So-and-so did this or forgot to do that. We would discuss how to handle the latest problem. Then one day I asked her what she thought the quality department contributes to the organization's Vision."

"Interesting, what was her answer?" Jean was pouring the coffee that I had brought over.

"She said her department contributed quality standards. So I asked who she helped. That was harder for her. She thought the company's customer was who she was helping."

Jean sat back in her chair and took a sip of coffee. "So what did you say to her then?"

"I asked her to use the Vision Development Chart to develop a Vision for the quality department."

Jean smiled. "I bet that was not easy for her."

"Well, actually it was kind of funny. The next morning Lisa was waiting for me. She was standing outside my office. I barely said good morning and she was telling me about this program and that plan and how she was going to handle the latest problem." Jean was smiling and nodding her head as I went on. "Yes, and in the process she discovered that our employees were her customers. Once she realized that, there was no stopping her," I laughed.

"Do you mind sharing her Vision for the quality department?" asked Jean.

"Not at all. The Quality Department provides guidance and education that creates a culture of compliance and a standard of performance that all employees live and expect of each other."

Jean was smiling. "I like that. It answers all the questions. Who are they: the Quality Department. What do they do: create a culture of compliance and standards. Why do they do it: so that employees understand and comply with quality regulations. How do they do it: through guidance and education."

"The Vision for her department has been a great tool for both of us," I said.

"Oh, how so?" asked Jean.

"We had an incident with contamination and no one was taking responsibility. There was a lot of finger pointing and excuses. Lisa was really having trouble sorting through it all. The information that Lisa had gathered pointed to people purposely not complying with a particular procedure. But she was having trouble deciding how to correct the problem."

Jean set her cup down. "Sounds complicated. How did you sort through all that?"

"I asked Lisa if she thought people chose not to comply or if the procedure was not usable. The way I saw it, we either had a problem with compliance or with the procedure. I explained that if it was a compliance problem, we had a trust or value issue and the person responsible would have to be terminated. However, if people did not understand why the procedure was needed, we had an assumption issue. If people did understand the purpose for the procedure we had a priority issue. If the cause of the contamination was due to assumption or priority issues, there was a problem with the procedure."

"What did Lisa say to that?" asked Jean.

"Lisa and I discussed what questions really needed to be asked. When Lisa felt more comfortable discussing the problem with the people involved, she was able to cut through the excuses and blame. Turns out, the procedure that had been put in place was not easy to comply with. In fact, people had been bypassing the procedure for some time. We were just lucky this had not happened before. We did not have to fire anyone and people learned that when something is not working, it is their responsibility to bring it to Lisa's attention.

Jean smiled. "It is much easier for individuals to contribute when they believe that what the organization does is important and what they personally contribute is needed. And you knew exactly what, when and how to communicate that."

I looked over at Jenkins who was licking his ears. "Hear that Jenkins? I finally learned to communicate. Couldn't have done it without you! Thanks!"

"John?" Jean was looking over her glasses at me.

I had seen that look many times before. Preparing myself for another story I asked, "Yes Jean?"

"You do know Jenkins can't really talk," Jean said with a sly little grin on her face.

"Well that may be," I said. "But I'd be careful what you say around him. He understands more than you think." I gave Jean a hug.

It was not until I reached my patio and turned to wave goodbye to Jean that I noticed Jenkins was following me. Jean was laughing. "It seems Jenkins has decided you're a leader worth following!"

# Quick Tips in a Nutshell

So, how does this work in the real world? Let's take the example of a young drug formulation company. Their focus was on research and development of a targeted delivery system that would reduce the toxicity of many of the drugs currently on the market. This company had successfully proven its potential with one customer and realized they needed an experienced CFO to help the company grow.

They took the time to discuss and agree on the responsibilities, characteristics and qualities they needed in a CFO. They wrote a job description describing the contributions that the CFO would be expected to make. They interviewed several candidates and hired an individual who came highly recommended and had a great deal of experience in growing young companies but had never worked with a company whose focus was scientific research and development.

Orientation and training were provided and included the company's vision which was:

"Formulation Company" is a biotechnology company providing the pharmaceutical industry with innovative formulation solutions for improved drug delivery. The COO explained that while their technology was novel, it was not "one size fits all". The nature of each compound they are trying to formulate requires a slight variation of the formulation. Therefore the research phase of every project is unpredictable and is always subject to change.

The CEO explained that it is also assumed that business procedures are there to provide a framework and support for every phase of research and development.

To succeed, the new CFO would need to gain a wider understanding of their research and development procedures, which is in part, dictated by federal regulatory requirements. Understanding the overall procedures would enable the new CFO to anticipate, respond to and provide pertinent financial information to management and the scientific R & D team.

Three months into the job, the CEO and the COO meet with the CFO to hear his recommendations for improving the financial systems and positioning the company for expansion and growth. The CFO had completed an historical look at spending to date and presented his recommendations for cost savings as well as a plan for projecting cash flow on a weekly basis. Then the discussion turned to new projects and potential new business. The COO was concerned that without an improved project management system there was no way to properly manage the costs of multiple projects. The CFO stated that he believed the company would benefit from discussions about financial consequences before changes to research studies were made. It was decided that the CFO and COO would revise the project management procedure to be more responsive and timely in capturing financial information throughout every phase of a project.

During one of their project management meetings, the COO asked the CFO what he meant when he said the company would benefit from discussions about financial consequences before changes in research studies were made. The CFO responded that it would help him write a better procedure if he understood why so many changes occur during the research phase of a project. Hoping that sitting in on some of the scientific discussions might help the CFO's understanding, the COO invited the CFO to the next research department meeting. The CFO attended the meeting and asked a lot of questions, thanked them for including him, that he gained a lot of information and would like to participate in more of these meetings.

The CFO attended every research meeting he could. He always asked a lot of questions and began to challenge many of the scientific decisions being made. Over time, the scientists resented his involvement and began questioning why he was invited to these meetings. The COO went to the CEO and reported his concern that the new CFO was trying to control costs by questioning and influencing the scientific decisions rather than focusing on financial and project management procedures.

QUICK TIPS IN A NUTSHELL

A month later, when the CEO expected to see a revised project management procedure, the CFO appeared frustrated and stated that the procedure was not finished. When the CEO asked why, the CFO responded that he is disappointed in the organization's lack of recognition of the financial limitations of the business and looked directly at the COO.

The COO responded, "You and I recognized the need for the finances to be captured in a more timely fashion. I have invited you, and you have participated in, numerous research meetings. The results of scientific studies are not predictable and dictate how the research will proceed. We have had many discussions about the research and development process. I was hoping that with your experience and understanding of business finance, you would provide more insight into how to capture the financial information needed.

Later that day the CEO invited the CFO to his office and said, "I have done an assessment of your performance to date. Would you care to see where I think there is room for improvement?"

The CEO handed the Assessment Form to the CFO and said, "as you can see, at this point in time, my assessment of your performance is barely at job level. That is not acceptable. I need you to be committed to, and take responsibility for, our vision."

|  | Trust | Assumptions | Priorities | Values |
|---|---|---|---|---|
| | "Company's" Goal | What "Company" Does | Why "Company" Does It | How "Company" Does It |
| **Commitment** — **Job Description** | | | | |
| | X | X | X | X |
| | Individual's Goal | What Individual Wants | Why Individual Does It | How Individual Does It |

77

"I am hoping that we have an assumption and/or priority issue so I would like to clarify a couple of assumptions. It has been my assumption that you would take on the responsibility of establishing financial procedures and providing the financial information needed for the organization to succeed. To date, you have identified the needs but you have not provided any answers. This morning you stated that you are frustrated by the organization's lack of recognition of the financial limitations. That statement is interpreted, by me, as an excuse. You blame the COO for not taking responsibility. But your job description clearly states that these responsibilities are yours."

The CEO went on to say, "Our success is based on successful scientific research. The formulation development process defines the scientific requirements needed for drug approval, which in turn, dictates financial requirements, not the other way around. Business functions support formulation development by providing procedures and generating data that allows the company to make focused, intelligent business decisions. The commitments as described in the CFO Job Description include: monitoring actual performance against budget for the product development phase of projects; providing financial analysis and perspective and direction for day-to-day operation as well as strategic decision making; developing budgets for additional product development and business development strategy. These are very high level responsibilities that require a wider perspective of the organization. It is not necessary or required for you to evaluate scientific results or the need for scientific studies. Understanding the scientific results will come with time. Understanding the process will help you anticipate, respond to and provide pertinent information and support the scientific development team."

The CEO closed by asking, "Has this been helpful? Is there anything that you need from me? Will you deliver the completed Project Management Procedure by Tuesday next week?"

A week later the CEO went to the CFO's office and asked to see the completed Project Management Procedure. The CFO stated that it was not quite finished. The CEO quickly determined that there was a trust issue and terminated the CFO. Why? How did he know he had a trust issue?

Trust can be the most difficult behavior to identify and the most uncomfortable issue to deal with. However, trust issues will undermine the leader's authority, create division within the organization and ultimately bring the organization down.

# QUICK TIPS IN A NUTSHELL

When trust is present in a relationship, people do what they said they will do. You know you can depend on them. Sounds simple, so why is it so difficult to identify trust behaviors? Because people create excuses and blame. Now, it is true, that upon occasion it is someone else's fault. People are not always responsible for another person's actions. But if leadership uses this excuse to not confront a trust issue, people will lose confidence in the leader. So, what are the behaviors that clearly exhibit a lack of trust?

1. Deliver the wrong thing.

Promise one thing - deliver something different. It is true that upon occasion situations occur that are out of our control. But people who are truly committed to the organization's assumptions will anticipate problems, confront issues and find ways to deliver what is needed. If someone consistently delivers the wrong final product, there is no commitment – there is no trust.

2. Late delivery.

People who agree to a timeline and do not adhere to the timeline, slow the process, or deliver late more than 10% of the time are not committed to the organizations' priorities. People who are committed to the organization's priorities will accept what is most important and make decisions that will ensure on time delivery.

3. Degrading/undermining the plan.

People who agree to a plan but find every opportunity to degrade or undermine the plan are not committed to the organization. This behavior is subversive and is often the most difficult to observe. People will engage in this behavior in unofficial meetings and behind your back. They may bring up issues that are not relevant to the discussion. They are the people who can always find a reason why something will not work and then find a way to prove they were right.

4. People unwilling to work with an individual or department. A person, who other people do not want to work with, is not committed to the organizations values. This person has blamed others so often that no one trusts them. They are not living the organization's values and if they are allowed to continue abusing other people, people will lose trust in leadership. The CEO has observed:

- The CFO blamed the COO for not recognizing the financial limitations of the business.

- The R & D scientists resented the CFO's involvement in the R & D meetings and began questioning why he was invited to these meetings.

- The CFO missed 3 delivery dates.

The CEO fired the CFO saying, "You and I have had many discussions about the research and development process and the needs of the organization. I was hoping that with your experience and understanding of business finance you would develop the financial procedures and documentation that would help grow our company. However, I no longer trust that you can deliver what is expected. It is time to terminate your employment with our Company. Please see HR for the necessary termination documents."

Of course, all kinds of behaviors occurred during the CFO's employment, many discussions had occurred and personal relationships had begun to develop. The CFO had come with remarkable references and high praise. He was a very personable individual, likable, the kind of guy you would enjoy having a beer with after work. But 3 of the 4 work behaviors indicated there was a trust issue. Because all communication had revolved around the Company's Vision, and assumptions, priorities and values had been clearly defined, action could be taken quickly and confidently.

## DISCUSSION QUESTIONS:

What was the message that everyone else in the organization heard when the CFO was terminated?

What is the message that everyone else in the organization would hear if the CFO was not terminated?

# About the Author

Jean Yarger is an educator, wife, mother, author, avid gardener with over 25 years experience in business administration and human resources. It was her experience as co-founder of a Wisconsin based pharmaceutical company that caused Jean to become passionate about helping people learn to succeed through other people. As Jean puts it, "You can have the most innovative new idea in the world, but the minute your success is determined by how other people perform, your passion becomes people."

Jean recognized that her company's management team was comprised of highly trained, intelligent professionals who were deficient in the skills needed to create success through people. There was no continuity or respect between departments. The performance assessment program hindered rather than facilitated real-time behavioral changes and no one was willing to put their personal goals aside for the organizations success.

Jean tried the standard means for improving management's leadership skills, but none of it seemed to identify the real issues or change behavior. Then Jean observed the "critters" in her garden communicating so simply – so effectively. It occurred to her that the issues, problems and critters in her garden were the same issues, problems and people in her organization. The difference being that in the garden, the issues seemed less confusing and performance problems were more easily addressed. Why? Because excuses and blame where not allowed and everyone knew what was important, why it was important and how they were going to keep it important.

## MORNINGS WITH JENKINS

*Mornings with Jenkins, the Tale of a Successful Leader* is the compilation of all the people, managers, issues and experiences Jean has encountered over the years. It is the tale of people we have all worked with and the individual who learns to lead them.

Ms. Yarger is currently the Chief Administrative Officer of ENDECE, LLC, a biotech drug discovery and development company and, second company co-founded by Jean and her husband. In addition to her duties as CAO Jean consults with business leaders, individuals and organizations looking to increase their influence and effectively lead with confidence.

Jean is the mother of two sons, has one granddaughter and loves sitting in her garden with her husband of 37 years.

www.ingramcontent.com/pod-product-compliance
Lightning Source LLC
Chambersburg PA
CBHW030910180526
45163CB00004B/1781